MW01065100

Collection Analysis
for the School Library
Media Center:
A Practical Approach

Carol A. Doll
and
Pamela Petrick Barron

AMERICAN LIBRARY ASSOCIATION
Chicago and London 1991

Designed by Luis Ramirez

Composed by Digital Graphics, Inc.
in Times Roman using the TEX
typesetting language, and output on
a DP-TEK 600 plain paper typesetter

Printed on 50-pound Finch Opaque, a
pH-neutral stock, and bound in
10-point Carolina cover stock
by Imperial Printing Company

The paper used in this publication meets the minimum requirements of American National Standard for Information Sciences—Permanence of Paper for Printed Library Materials, ANSI Z39.48–1984. ∞

Single copies of figures may be reproduced without permission.

Library of Congress Cataloging-in-Publication Data
Doll, Carol Ann, 1949–
    Collection analysis for the school library media center : a
practical approach / Carol A. Doll and Pamela Petrick Barron.
        p. cm.
    Includes bibliographical references.
    ISBN 0-8389-3390-4
    1. School libraries–Collection development. 2. Media programs
(Education) I. Barron, Pamela Petrick. II. Title.
Z675.S3D598 1990
025.2'188–dc20   90-40208

Printed in the United States of America.

95 94 93 92 91   5 4 3 2 1

Contents

Introduction

THE PURPOSE OF this book is to introduce you to a technique for gathering information about your collection and then using this information to make informed decisions about your collection. By using the data generated from this technique, librarians have been able to obtain additional funding for their libraries.

This technique has been used successfully in South Carolina by school library media specialists for the past six years. It can easily be adapted to other library settings. Library media specialists in a Florence School District were able to get a bond referendum passed, and media specialists in Charleston conducted a district-wide analysis that convinced administrators that additional funding was needed. After presenting a workshop to a group of school media specialists on the South Carolina coast, a school district administrator told the authors that he could endorse their technique because it gave him some solid evidence for making decisions about allocating funds to media centers.

The authors wish to acknowledge the help received from a colleague, Dan Barron. It was his idea to have his school library administration students examine school library collections, including the elementary school library collection where I was the media specialist. That action enabled us to expand upon and develop the ideas presented in this book. Dan's students are still collecting these statistics today. Because of his and their efforts, there is a clearer understanding of the state of school library media center collections in South Carolina, and prospective and practicing school library media specialists are learning to apply research techniques effectively.

Carol Doll regularly teaches this technique to students in her class on services to children and young adults in public libraries.

In this volume we present our ideas in a cookbook approach. We provide the recipe; you supply your own ingredients. Do not be dismayed to discover mathematical calculations and statistics. You *can* do it! Just take one step at a time. Fill in the blanks on the forms and before you know it, you will have gathered some data that you can use to your advantage.

We would like to hear from you. Please let us know what you accomplish.

Good luck!

PAMELA PETRICK BARRON

Selected
Quotes

The single most important activity for building the knowledge required for the eventual success in reading is reading aloud to children (both parents and teachers).

Becoming a Nation of Readers, p. 23

Schools should maintain well-stocked and managed libraries. Access to interesting and informative books is one of the keys to a successful reading program.

Becoming a Nation of Readers, p. 119

As important as an adequate collection of books is a librarian who encourages wide reading and helps match books to children.

Becoming a Nation of Readers, p. 119

Children improve their reading ability by reading a lot. Reading achievement is directly related to the amount of reading children do in school and outside.

What Works: Research about Teaching and Learning, p. 11

Books should be part of every child's life. They should occupy a central place in home and classroom alike. Children should have at their fingertips books like *Where the Wild Things Are, Charlotte's Web*, and *Winnie the Pooh*. This is the only way they will really grasp the idea that reading is a joy rather than a burden . . . . One thing that may turn children away from reading is the dubious quality of their other textbooks.

First Lessons: A Report on Elementary Education in America, p. 24

ONE

Management Objectives

What Is a Collection Analysis?

AS LIBRARIANS, we are well aware of the wide range of services we make available to our patrons. Central to these services is the development of a collection of materials upon which we and our patrons will draw. Collection development is the process by which the library staff acquires a wide range of materials to meet the needs of its patrons. According to Evans, there are six definable elements in collection development: (1) community analysis, (2) policies, (3) selection, (4) acquisition, (5) weeding, and (6) evaluation.[1] Thus collection evaluation or analysis is just one aspect of collection development, and is the focus of this book.

The purpose of a collection analysis is to determine the quality of the collection. Quality may be measured in numerous ways. Underlying the notion of quality is *management*, the effective combination of resources to achieve a desired outcome.

The vocabulary of management principles includes the following terms: systematic, measurable, efficient, effective, input, output, inner environment, and outer environment. Almost all of the systematic management techniques or methods contain these elements: the systematic allocation of resources, an evaluation of their effectiveness, and the ability to communicate both need and effectiveness of resource allocation to all of those involved in the process.[2]

Evaluation of a library collection usually falls into two categories: the evaluation of the collection itself, usually in terms of numbers, quality, currency, or similar measures, and (perhaps most important) how well the collection serves the needs of the community. Because meeting the needs of the library's users is so impor-

1

tant, any collection analysis should include a needs assessment, that is, an analysis of the community that the library serves, including current and future users.[3] We need to know where we are before we can know where we are going.

Determining where we are in our collections can be difficult partly because of the ways collections have been measured. For example, references to recommended collection size can be misleading, for size alone does not guarantee that the appropriate items will be included. *Information Power: Guidelines for School Library Media Programs* addresses this point:

> Adequacy of the collection size is best determined through an evaluation of how well the collection and information services are meeting the needs of the users. Criteria that can be applied to assess the adequacy of collection size include determining whether the collection is large enough to satisfy a certain percentage of requests, whether it represents basic titles and sources recommended in standard selection tools, and whether, as judged by users themselves, it offers sufficient materials to stimulate and promote literacy development and to support special program emphases. An overriding concern must be for the recency of the information contained in the materials.[4]

This document also provides helpful suggestions about what issues should be addressed in collection development:

> All schools must have a collection development plan that addresses their collection needs and includes such specific steps as school/community analysis, policy development, selection, acquisition, weeding, and evaluation.[5]

To follow these suggestions, a good way to begin a needs assessment is by asking the following questions: What is the *ideal* situation? What are the standards for our type of library? Are they based on traditional or contemporary views? What is *our ideal*? If we could have the library of our dreams, what would it be like? What is *our organization's mission statement and goals*? They should match our personal expectations. Lastly, what are the *expectations and needs* of our outer environment, the community that we serve? Do we understand and appreciate the expectations of our clientele? Are we responsive to their needs and do we plan accordingly?[6]

After we have asked these questions, the next step is to make an internal analysis of our resources, including all books, audiovisuals, and journals subscribed to and available from a library. There are several ways to analyze collections, such as focusing on gross numbers, like the overall total, or grouping the collection by classification numbers, or dividing the collection by subject areas, such as those used to support specific areas of a school's curriculum, or even dividing the number of items in the collection by the number of users or potential users to obtain a per capita figure. Collections are often analyzed and quantified by type of material, for example, reference, audiovisual, or special collections. Growth rates can be examined, such as the number of items added or deleted during a year. The expenditures for each type of material during a year may also be considered.

Collections are often compared to published standards for various types of libraries. Often these are only gross numbers, for example, a minimum of 10 books per pupil. The problem with these measures is that they are quantitative rather than qualitative evaluations. They tell you how much or how many, but convey little information concerning the quality of the collection.

To get a more qualitative analysis of your collection you could consider comparing your collection to selected lists, such as core collections, or bibliographies for special areas, such as science or college reading lists, or to current adopted textbooks' recommended "further reading" lists, such as those for a new reading series whose purpose is to give students additional practice or reinforcement. You may compare to teacher-generated or other published or recommended bibliographies, analyze by copyright dates (especially useful for more timely topics such as space flight), analyze by use or lack of use, or have the librarian decide. This last approach can be either systematic or impressionistic, for example, judging the physical condition of the material. A combination of these techniques can be helpful, depending upon your objectives. Some suggestions for employing these methods of analysis will be discussed at greater length in later chapters.

The collection is only one aspect of the internal analysis of a library. Other considerations are personnel, facilities, and user perceptions (their levels of satisfaction or frustration either through formal or informal statements). This analysis must also include a community analysis. What kind of community do you serve? What about potential users? What kinds of external resources are there, such as other libraries, museums, agencies, institutions, business and industry? Consideration of all these elements is useful in preparing an effective collection development policy. Such policies are necessary because they provide guidelines for choosing items for the collection.

One important aspect of analysis that is sometimes overlooked is a personal analysis. You need to put yourself into the picture. What are your career goals? Are you satisfied with the quality of your life? What about your health, both emotional and physical? What about your intellectual and spiritual growth? Are your needs being met? If not, why not? We are well aware of how personal satisfaction affects our job performance. This needs to be taken into consideration.

After you have examined all of these elements, you know where you are and you are ready to develop objectives. By setting and focusing on objectives, you have a plan or a path to follow. You can begin to chart progress. Objectives may fall under daily operations, problem solving, innovation or research, or personal growth and development.

A word of caution when developing objectives and setting goals. We are often our own worst enemies. We sometimes set goals that take a long time to reach or are impossible to attain or difficult to measure. This causes us to become frustrated. We do need to set some long-term goals, but we must also set some objectives that we can attain in a shorter period of time. This allows us to build in our own reward system, to have some positive experiences, to feel good about ourselves, and to continue to strive toward our long-term goals.

After setting our goals and creating objectives, including some that can be measured, we need to develop strategies to meet them. This is a wonderful opportunity to allow the free flow of ideas and to consider alternatives. You might want to try some brainstorming just to bring in some fresh perspectives. In developing these strategies, the normal constraints of personnel, training, time, hard and soft money, and the effects on clients and personnel must be taken into consideration to develop realistic strategies.

The last step is communication and public relations. You need to communicate your goals and objectives to both your inner and outer environment. You need support, encouragement, and involvement from both if reaching your goals is to become a reality.

Why Do a Collection Analysis?

Now that you have an understanding of all the elements that need to be considered in a needs assessment, you may be asking, So what? Why go to all that trouble? What will it accomplish? We have presented the theoretical foundations, but we also know that the approach does work in practice. One of the authors' own experiences as a building level media specialist will be used to illustrate how you can put theory into practice.

Six years ago, Pam Barron was the new and the only media specialist at an elementary school in a school district near Columbia, South Carolina. Dan Barron, a professor at the College of Library and Information Science at the University of South Carolina, sent two of his school library administration students out to the elementary school to draw a statistical sampling of the collection.

Based on this sample, the students determined that the average age of the collection was 22.66 years. They also compared this sample to the titles found in Phase 1 of the *Elementary School Library Collection* and discovered that the collection contained only 9.96 percent of the recommended titles.

Until this sample was drawn, the media specialist had sensed that the collection was woefully inadequate, but had no hard data to support this feeling. Building on the students' findings, the media specialist gathered additional statistics. She determined the number of titles needed and the amount of funds needed to purchase the remainder of the Phase 1 books. Since a new reading series had just been adopted by the district, she checked to see how many of the supplementary books listed in the series for additional reading practice were in her library's collection. In addition, she isolated one topic, space flight, to examine in greater detail. The results were abysmal.

For example, there were eight titles with the subject heading Space Flight, and their copyright dates were as follows:

1959	1 title
1961	1 title
1963	1 title
1964	1 title
1965	4 titles

This was 1984. Human beings walked on the moon in 1969, but according to the books in this library, they were still trying to get there.

Of the 718 titles listed in the reading series as supplementary books, 56 were in this library's collection. We know that often text books do not have librarians on their advisory committees, nor are the materials listed always the most recent. Sometimes these lists include only current titles. Still, 56 out of 718 titles are a poor result.

These data were used to prepare a report for the building level principal. This information was also used by the school's advisory committee to make recommendations to the district administrators.

In this school district, each school's budget request was based on recommendations made by its advisory committee. This school's advisory committee recommended that the library's collection be the school's top priority.

After this recommendation was made, Barron compiled a one-page report and made an appointment to talk with the district's assistant superintendent. The actual report that was submitted is presented as Figure 1.

The length of the report is important. Administrators are extremely busy and are more willing to give their attention to reports that are concise and that present a clear analysis of the situation. A great deal of information was conveyed to the administrator on

---

Status of Book Collection at _____

The book collection at _____ was analyzed to

1. Determine the age of the collection.
2. Determine the quality of the current collection by making a comparison of titles we have to the titles that should be on the shelves of media centers serving grades K–5. The *Elementary School Library Collection*, a highly regarded selection source, was used to make the comparison.

Results

1. The present collection is 22.66 years old on the average.
2. It contains 9.96 percent of the titles that should be on the shelves of elementary school media centers.

Cost to Upgrade the Collection to Minimum

Nonfiction and Fiction Books	1,746 titles	cost $12,978.15
Picture Books	687 titles	cost 4,926.76
Total	2,433 titles	cost $17,904.91

Memos

1. The cost of the books listed above reflects the purchase of one copy of a book per title. It does not take into account that multiple copies of some titles would be necessary.
2. These numbers reflect the minimum number of titles that should be included based on recommendations. They do not take into account the supplementary books that are listed for our reading series nor the special collections like the South Carolina books. At present we have 56 of the 718 supplementary books listed for the reading series.
3. Analysis of reference books shows we have 16.67 percent of the minimum number of recommended titles. These books were not included in the costs listed above.

Figure 1. Report to a District Administrator

this single page. As a result of this report, the administrator decided that additional funding was necessary and assured Barron that steps would be taken before the next school year.

When Barron returned from summer vacation, she discovered that the administration had given her an additional $1,000. Since she needed almost $8,000, she was, of course, badly disappointed. Still she had one thousand more dollars than she would have had if the report had not been written. Rather than give up, she decided to look for additional funding sources.

When school budgets began shrinking over the last decade, schools started looking elsewhere for funds. One major source of funds for schools has been the business sector. It has become a common practice for schools to form partnerships with local businesses. The businesses adopt the schools and provide them with a variety of resources, ranging from actual products of the company to cash donations. Unfortunately there were no businesses in this particular school's community that were large enough to lend support. Nor were there any foundations or other philanthropic agencies.

One possible source was the South Carolina State Department of Education. Because of declining test scores, the citizens of South Carolina had agreed to a one-cent sales tax increase to raise funds for education. Also under the terms of the Education Improvement Act (EIA, 1984), grants as large as $5,000 for innovative educational programs, called school improvement grants, were available.

Barron remembered reading an article entitled, "The Effect of Literature on Vocabulary and Reading Achievement,"[7] which described a study that had been done to improve the reading skills of children using children's literature. There were many similarities between the student population in the study and Barron's student population, such as a high percentage of students reading below grade level, low socio-economic level, and a large minority population. The major difference between these two groups was location. The students in the study were from a large urban area, New York City; the students in the school were in a more rural area. The elementary school seemed to present a perfect opportunity to replicate the study in a different location. Thus Barron gathered statistics to describe her student population, and she used them in her grant application. She wrote:

> The evidence or need for special emphasis in reading can be found by considering the following background information. Our student body is composed of 402 students in grades K-5. Forty-four per-

cent (44%) are reading below grade level. Chapter 1 tutors serve twenty percent (200%). Fifty-five percent (55%) are on free or reduced lunch and thirty-three percent (33%) are from minority groups. While traditional means for teaching reading are good and may meet with some success, many of our students are victims of language impoverishment, due in part to lack of exposure to books. To improve students' reading skills additional strategies for exposing children to books need to be explored.

She submitted a grant proposal, "The Impact of Reading Aloud to 1st, 2nd, 3rd, 4th, and 5th Graders on BSAP and CTBS Scores." These scores are the results of standardized tests used in South Carolina, the Basic Skills Assessment Program (BSAP) and the Comprehensive Test of Basic Skills (CTBS). Figure 2 is a statement of the goals and objectives of the study.

The grant proposal was accepted and the entire grant of $5,000 was used to purchase library books. Ten teachers and 215 students representing two classes for each grade from one to five participated. In each grade level, one class listened to reading aloud for at least 20 minutes per day; the other class did not.

At the end of the grant period, an evaluation was made. Test scores had increased. More importantly, this process fostered a greater interest in reading as shown by increased circulation of library books. It also demonstrated to students that they could have pleasurable experiences with books. This observation was based on written responses collected from the participants, both students and teachers. Because of the way grant funds were administered by the South Carolina State Department of Education, the study period was only seven weeks. Barron felt that further study was warranted and the proposal was resubmitted for the following school year. It was funded a second time, and an additional $5,000 was used to purchase library books.

While these grant projects were being conducted, Barron, using the data generated from the collection analysis, was able to get $4,000 for library books from the school's PTA. Thus one collection analysis was used to generate $15,000 additional funding, a good payoff for a few hours in work gathering statistics.

South Carolina has other success stories. Betty Ann Smith, a media specialist in Florence School District 1, effectively used the data gathered from a collection analysis. A news story headlined "School Library Collections Have Outdated Books," in which Mrs. Smith was interviewed, appeared in the *Florence Morning News* on May 3, 1988. It attracted so much publicity that voters passed a bond referendum for library books.

The Impact of Reading Aloud to 1st, 2nd, 3rd, 4th, and 5th
Graders on BSAP and CTBS Scores

The purpose of this proposed project is to implement strategies from a successful project conducted in New York City in 1968 which involved elementary school children who had academic retardation, low socio-economic levels, and a high percentage of racial minorities. The focus of that project was "to find an approach to the problems of poor motivation and inadequate readiness that would stimulate children's desire to achieve competency in reading while strengthening their desire to do so."[1]

Reading aloud of children's literature was chosen as the appropriate solution to the problem because previous research conducted with children had demonstrated that adults can enhance children's ability to read independently by reading books aloud to them. Results of the project demonstrated that reading aloud to children had a positive effect on word knowledge, quality of vocabulary, and reading comprehension as evidenced by significant improvement on reading achievement test scores. The primary goal of this project is to determine what impact reading aloud to classes of 1st, 2nd, 3rd, 4th, and 5th graders has on their BSAP and CTBS scores.

Measurable outcomes of this project will include:

1. By the end of this project the grantee will develop, use, evaluate, and prepare a list of books that would be appropriate for reading aloud to each of the grades from one to five.
2. By the end of the school year, children in the classes that were read aloud to on a regular basis, will show an increase in either their BSAP of CTBS scores over those in the classes that were not.

References
1. Dorothy H. Cohen, "The Effect of Literature on Vocabulary and Reading Achievement" in *Jump over the Moon: Selected Professional Readings* by Pamela Petrick Barron and Jennifer O. Burley. New York: Holt, Rinehart, and Winston, 1984, p. 434–41.

Figure 2. Statement of Goals and Objectives in a Grant Proposal

Peggy Hanna, School Library Media Coordinator for the Charleston School District, encouraged all of her media specialists to draw statistical samplings of their collections to calculate the average age. She also told them to select one area of the curriculum for a more thorough analysis. The statistics generated were compiled in a report to the district's administrators. As a result, the libraries obtained additional funding.

These success stories should pique your interest. The remainder of this book will be devoted to explaining how to draw a sample from your collections and use the data generated to obtain support for your libraries.

A great deal of national attention and concern has focused on education and literacy. *A Nation at Risk* helped arouse national concern about American education.[8] The year 1990 was designated as International Literacy Year. As librarians, we are fortunate to be living in a time when the emphasis in reading instruction is shifting to the use of children's literature. The professional literature can help you obtain additional funding for children's books. A sampling of these sources is included in the Selected Readings.

Notes

1. G. Edward Evans, *Developing Library and Information Center Collections*, 2d ed. (Littleton, Colo. Libraries Unlimited, 1987), p. 14.
2. Daniel D. Barron, College of Library and Information Science, University of South Carolina. Unpublished lecture notes.
3. Evans, p. 14.
4. American Association of School Librarians and Association for Educational Communications and Technology, *Information Power: Guidelines for School Library Media Programs* (Chicago: American Library Association; Washington, D.C.: Association for Educational Communications and Technology, 1988), p. 72.
5. *Information Power*, p. 73.
6. Charles Curran and F. W. Summers, *Library Performance, Accountability, and Responsiveness* (Norwood, N.J.: Ablex, 1990), p. 149–51.
7. Dorothy H. Cohen, "The Effect of Literature on Vocabulary and Reading Achievement" in *Jump over the Moon—Selected Professional Readings*, edited by Pamela Petrick Barron and Jennifer Q. Burley (New York: Holt, Rinehart and Winston, 1984), p. 434–41.
8. *A Nation at Risk*, National Commission on Excellence in Education (Washington, D.C.: Government Printing Office, 1983).

Selected Readings

Becoming a Nation of Readers: The Report of the Commission on Reading. National Institute of Education and the Center for the Study of Reading, 1985.

Bennett, William G. *First Lessons: A Report on Elementary Education in America*. U.S. Department of Education, September 1986.

Cullinan, Bernice E. "Latching on to Literature: Reading Initiatives Take Hold." *School Library Journal*, April 1989, p. 27–31.

Evans, G. Edward. *Developing Library and Information Center Collections*, 2d ed. Littleton, Colo.: Libraries Unlimited, 1987.

Fisher, Carol J., and Barbara Elleman. "The Read-Aloud Remedy." *Instructor*, January 1984, p. 66–68.

Hoffman, April. "Families That Read Together Overcome Rift." *American Libraries*, October 1985, p. 647–49.

Stahlschmidt, Agnes D. "The Library Media Specialist and the Read-Aloud Program." *School Library Media Quarterly*, Winter 1984, p. 146–49.

Task Force on Reading Improvement: A Report on Improving Reading in South Carolina. September 1986.

Van Orden, Phyllis J. *The Collection Program in Schools: Concepts, Practices, and Information Sources.* Englewood, Colo.: Libraries Unlimited, 1988.

What Works: Research about Teaching and Learning. U.S. Department of Education, 1986.

TWO

Data Analysis

Sampling the Collection

A LIBRARY COLLECTION consists of books, journals, films, film-strips, pamphlets and other items. If that collection is to be evaluated, the total number of items can be overwhelming. It is neither necessary nor practical to evaluate every item in the collection. Instead, a small portion of the total collection can and should be used, if that smaller portion is properly selected. This smaller portion, called a sample, can be used to make generalizations about the entire collection.

For the researcher or librarian to make valid inferences about the entire collection, the sample must be representative. That is, the sample must be carefully chosen so it contains all of the characteristics of the library collection and so that those characteristics are present in the same quantity and quality as in the collection itself. For example, if 49 percent of the collection is fiction, then 49 percent of the sample titles should be fiction.

The common method of obtaining a representative sample is to select it randomly. This ensures that every item in the collection has an equal chance of being selected for the sample. Three techniques for obtaining random samples will be discussed later.

Of course, it is impossible for every sample to be a small-scale copy of the collection. Checking a sample of two hundred titles is just not the same as checking every title in the collection. Some differences occur when random samples are selected. For example, if a fair coin is tossed ten times, it would be reasonable to predict five heads and five tails. But an actual trial might result in six heads and four tails, or eight heads and two tails. These deviations, called sampling error, that occur when a *random* sample is being selected are due entirely to chance. If the sample is randomly chosen, statistical methods can compensate for sampling error. But they cannot correct for any bias that arises if random sampling is not used. For example, a media specialist may eliminate titles from the sample if she dislikes the author or intends to weed that book shortly. Such bias would adversely affect the final results. Random sampling uses a totally neutral method to identify sample titles. Applied to a random sample, the techniques described in this book can be used with confidence.

Sampling error decreases as sample size increases. One may toss ten heads in a row when using a fair coin. It is much less likely to toss a fair coin and get one hundred heads in a row. For the techniques described here, a sample size of two hundred titles is recommended. This is large enough to provide useful results (it has been used successfully by this researcher in numerous studies) and it is a manageable size.

When selecting a random sample, the first step is to decide what part of the collection is to be evaluated, for example, circulating items, fiction, nonfiction, nonbook media, periodicals, reference works, or vertical file materials.

Once the librarian or media specialist decides what items are to be evaluated, a listing of the items where each item is equally represented must be identified. For example, the shelflist can be used, when one is available, because there each title is included once, under the main entry, whereas in the card catalog a title may have multiple entries. In a divided card catalog, the title section would be the best alternative if a shelflist is not available. Some automated circulation systems can generate a list of all titles in their files, and the printout can be used like a shelflist. The sample may be taken directly from the shelves if (1) the volumes are counted, not measured (thicker volumes have a greater chance of being selected), and (2) an appropriate proportion of items in circulation is included. (See Stratified Random Sampling below.)

Three methods for selecting a random sample will be discussed here: simple random sampling, stratified random sampling, and systematic random sampling. All three are valid techniques. The most appropriate technique to use depends on the collection and the purpose of the evaluation.

SIMPLE RANDOM SAMPLING

In this uncomplicated technique, the sample is drawn from the population in such a way that every possible sample of the selected size has the same chance of being chosen. Drawing numbers from a hat or pulling marbles from a jar of equal sized marbles are examples of simple random sampling.

To draw a sample

1. Identify all members of the library collection from which the sample will be selected. It may be helpful to number the items.
2. *Randomly* select the titles for the sample.

To randomly select the sample, a variety of methods can be used. Tables of random numbers, generated by computer, may be found in math or statistics texts or as separate volumes. These tables can be read in any direction and for as many digits as necessary. Numbers may also be drawn from a hat, or the last digits of phone numbers can be used. Lists of random numbers can also be generated by computer programs.

In some cases, dice can be helpful, but use them with caution. The familiar pair of six-sided dice does not permit random sampling. The number 1 never occurs, 2 or 12 can only happen in one way, but 1 and 6 or 2 and 5 or 3 and 4 all yield 7. Because each number is not equally likely, a pair of dice cannot be used to select a random sample. But some of the gaming dice for role-playing games have as many as 100 sides, and may work well for random sampling.

For an example of simple random sampling, imagine a collection of 12 titles and a sample of 4. Using a random number table, items 11, 2, 9, and 6 were selected for the sample.

```
    X          X
   (X)         X
    X         (X)
    X          X
    X         (X)
   (X)         X
```

Simple random sampling is the least complicated technique. With large collections, it can be unwieldy, and it will not always include members of all subgroups in the collection.

STRATIFIED RANDOM SAMPLING

If it is important for every subgroup to be proportionally represented in the sample, use the stratified random sampling technique. In this case, a sample is obtained by separating the collection into groups and selecting a proportionate simple random sample from each group.

To obtain a stratified random sample

1. Identify all items of the library collection to be evaluated.
2. Identify the various groups in the collection to be studied. For example, if all nonreference books in the collection are to be evaluated, and no shelflist or listing of the titles is available, the sample must be taken from books on the shelf and books in circulation.
3. Determine what proportion of the collection is found in each group. For example, you may find 25 percent of the titles are in circulation and 75 percent on the shelf.
4. Decide on the sample size. Two hundred titles is the recommended sample size. For purposes of this discussion, the collection consists of 12 books and the sample size is 4.
5. Calculate how many items of the sample should be allotted to each group. If 25 percent of the collection is in circulation, 25 percent of the sample, or one title, should be drawn from books currently checked out. And 75 percent of the sample, or three titles, should be drawn from books on the shelf.
6. Randomly select the indicated number of titles from each group using simple random sampling. According to a random number table, items 1, 2, and 9 from the first group and item 3 from the second group will be in the sample.

On the Shelf	In Circulation
Ⓧ	X
Ⓧ	X
X	Ⓧ
X	
X	
X	
X	
X	
Ⓧ	

Stratified random sampling guarantees that all subgroups within the collection, such as the Dewey classes, will be proportionately represented in the sample. But there are times, especially when some subgroups are large, that stratified random sampling also becomes unwieldy. If a list of items in the collection is available, systematic random sampling may be the easiest technique.

SYSTEMATIC RANDOM SAMPLING

Using this method, a sample is obtained by selecting items according to a predetermined sequence, such as every tenth book.

To use systematic random sampling

1. Identify all items in the library collection to be evaluated.
2. Determine the total number of such items in the collection. For purposes of this discussion, the collection size is 12.
3. Decide on the sample size. Again, two hundred is recommended. Four is used in this discussion.
4. Divide the total number of items by the desired sample size to find the interval size. Since $12 \div 4 = 3$, the interval in this example is 3.
5. Randomly select a starting point less than or equal to the interval. Using the last digits of phone numbers or dollar bill serial numbers can ensure randomness. In this example, the starting point is 2.
6. Starting at the beginning of the list, count to the starting point. That item is the first in the sample.
7. If that item is unacceptable (e.g., it is a reference book and only circulating titles are to be included), continue to the first acceptable item.
8. Add the interval size to the starting place to locate the second title. For example, if item 2 is the first title for the sample and the interval size is 3, then item 5 is the next title in the sample.
9. Continue until the end of the list is reached. Using this technique, items 2, 5, 8, and 11 will be included in the sample.

```
      X          X
     (X)        (X)
      X          X

      X          X
     (X)        (X)
      X          X
```

This technique can work well if an online circulation system can print a list of all titles in the database. Then systematic sampling can be used to sample from the entire list. Systematic random sampling may also be combined with either of the other two methods. For example, it may be easier to determine the number of pages in the printout than the number of titles listed. in that case, use systematic random sampling to identify pages and use simple random sampling (e.g., throw a role-playing die) to select specific titles.

If the computer printout of holdings is in call-nputer order, stratified random sampling may determine the proportionate number needed from each of the Dewey or LC classes. Then systematic random sampling may identify specific titles.

The advantage of systematic random sampling is that its orderly approach can be more efficient. If the starting point is selected randomly, the sample is also selected randomly.

To use systematic random sampling on a traditional card shelflist, follow these steps:

1. Measure the total length of the cards in the shelflist drawers in centimeters, an easier unit to add than fractions of inches. Hold the drawers horizontally and keep the tension fairly equal from drawer to drawer. (A shelflist measuring form is suggested in Figure 3.)
2. Decide on the size of the sample. Two hundred cards is the recommended size.
3. Divide the total shelflist length (the bottom line on the shelflist measuring form) by the sample size. The quotient is the interval size. For example, if the total shelflist length is 2,680 cm, the interval is $2,680 \div 200$ or 13.4 cm.
4. Randomly select a starting point less than or equal to the interval. For example, if the interval is 13.4 cm, a number less than or equal to 134 should be selected. The final digits of dollar bill serial numbers or telephone numbers can be used to ensure randomness. (Don't use telephone numbers you know; select unfamiliar ones from the telephone book.)
5. Beginning with the first drawer of the shelflist, measure to the starting point, and insert a straight pin from the side. Then count back five cards. The first acceptable card following the fifth card is the first title in the sample. (Older card stock is heavier. Because of wear, some cards are wider at the top than others. Sampling from the side and counting back five cards helps compensate for worn cards and heavier paper, and gives all titles an equal chance of being chosen.)

6. From the starting point, measure the length of the interval to locate the second title. Measure from the second title to find the third title, and so on. If the first title is at 9.9 cm and the interval is 13.4 cm, the second title is at 9.9 + 13.4 or 23.3 cm. The third title is at 23.3 + 13.4 or 36.7 cm.
7. At the end of one drawer, carry over the extra centimeters to the front of the next drawer and continue measuring intervals to the end of the shelflist.

When you have reached the end of the shelflist, it is wise to count how many titles are in the sample. Often, the actual sample

Category	Length
000s	_____
100s	_____
200s	_____
300s	_____
400s	_____
500s	_____
600s	_____
700s	_____
800s	_____
900s	_____
Biography	_____
	Total nonfiction _____
Fiction	_____
Easy Books	_____
Short stories	_____
	Total fiction _____
Reference	_____
Audiovisual	_____
Other	_____
	Total miscellaneous _____
	Total shelflist _____

Figure 3. Shelflist Measuring Form

size will be the same as the one selected, e.g., 200 titles. If there are, for example, only 197 cards, you may proceed with the collection analysis by using the number 197 instead of 200 in the calculations. Or you may randomly select a shelflist drawer, and then a location in centimeters (using phone numbers or dollar bill serial numbers) to obtain the additional titles.

Index cards should be used to record the titles in the sample, one title per card. It is much easier to shuffle and rearrange index cards than it is to handle a list of titles on sheets of paper. A format for information on the index card is suggested in Figure 4.

In Figure 3, it is not necessary to complete every blank. Use the applicable categories and skip the others. It may be appropriate to evaluate only some kinds of materials in the collection. For example, in order to emphasize the book collection, periodicals and audiovisual materials could be omitted. Or only reference books and materials for adult readers could be surveyed. Which portion of the collection is to be evaluated depends on the purpose of the survey and the professional judgment of the librarian or media specialist.

It is easiest and most efficient to take the random sample from the shelflist. But this is not always possible. If the catalog is divided, the sample may be drawn from the title cards following the procedure given for sampling the shelflist.

As more library collections become automated, fewer shelflists are available. However, each item in the computer has a unique number or identification code, similar to an acquisition number.

Author _____

Title _____

Call No. _____

Copyright Date _____

Listed in Standard Sources:

_____

_____

_____

_____

Last Due Date _____

Figure 4. Possible Format for Sample Card

Sometimes the computer can print out a list of these numbers or a list of titles held. If the identification numbers were assigned sequentially, and if the beginning and final numbers can be readily identified, then, apply the techniques for systematic random sampling.

If neither a computer listing nor a shelflist is available, the sample can be taken directly from the shelves and circulation file. As described before, divide the total collection size by the sample size to find the interval, randomly select a starting point less than or equal to the interval, and, beginning there, select titles separated by the interval, for example, every fourteenth book. Be sure to sample from books in circulation, too. If the circulation file is not accessible, sample from books returned over a period of time.

Data Analysis

The methods of collection evaluation can be either quantitative or qualitative. Quantitative methods attempt to determine collection quality by using numerical data, such as the number of titles in the collection or the average collection age. Qualitative methods attempt to measure the overall quality of the collection. Comparison to a bibliography of recommended titles or ability to meet user needs can estimate collection quality. Both quantitative and qualitative evaluation can be helpful in analyzing the collection, and both will be discussed here.

Once the shelflist has been measured and the random sample selected, a number of procedures can be followed to analyze the data. Several of these will be explained and discussed below. Any or all of these procedures may be appropriate in a given situation, and all of them provide additional information about the collection.

COLLECTION PERCENTAGES

It may be useful to know the proportion of titles in various categories or classes of the collection. From the information gathered in Figure 3, it is relatively easy to calculate the percent of titles in each category. Use Figure 3 to fill in the middle column of Figure 5. Then follow directions at the bottom of the figure.

David V. Loertscher has proposed a method of collection evaluation called mapping. Because this technique relates collection evaluation to the school's curriculum, it is responsive to local needs. Further work by Loertscher and Ho gives data on the percent of titles in different categories for both existing collections and bibliographies of recommended titles. These percentages could be compared with the figures obtained in Figure 5 to show whether the collection matches the standard data, is below the average in some areas, or is strong in some areas. This information should be used as a guide only. Collections should differ from standard or average data as they respond to local needs. School library media specialists must use their professional judgment. Why purchase extensive recommended geology materials if geology is not in the curriculum?

Dewey Class	Length in cm	Percent
000s	_____	_____
100s	_____	_____
200s	_____	_____
300s	_____	_____
400s	_____	_____
500s	_____	_____
600s	_____	_____
700s	_____	_____
800s	_____	_____
900s	_____	_____
Biography	_____	_____
Fiction	_____	_____
Easy Books	_____	_____
Short stories	_____	_____
Reference	_____	_____
Audiovisual	_____	_____

To calculate the percent for each category:
1. Multiply the number of centimeters in that category times 100.
2. Divide by the total number of centimeters in the shelflist. Use the total shelflist number from Figure 3.
3. Enter the result in the "Percent" column.

Figure 5. Calculating Collection Percentages

AVERAGE AGE OF COLLECTION

Another useful number is the average age of the collection. This is also relatively easy to calculate from the sample cards. Use Figure 6. (It may be necessary to include years earlier than 1971.) Follow the steps given below:

1. In the first blank column fill in the number of titles for each year. This may be easier if the sample cards are in chronological order or are first sorted into piles.
2. Fill in the next column. For example, for the year 1987, write 87. If the sample includes any titles dated 1900 or earlier, leave this column blank. You must use the entire date instead of only the last two digits.
3. For each line in the table, multiply the number of books by the last two digits of the year or the full date (see step 2) and write the product in the last column.
4. Add the products in the last column.
5. Divide this total by the number of titles in the sample. This gives the average copyright date of the sample. For example, if 63 is the result, the date is 1963. If 1921 is the result (for a collection including titles published before 1900), the average date is 1921.
6. Subtract the average copyright date from the current year to find the average age of the sample in years. For example, if the average copyright date is 1963 and the current year is 1992, the average age of the sample is 29 years. It is also a good estimate of the average age of the collection, if the proper procedure was used to obtain the sample.

For purposes of comparison, a random sample was taken from four retrospective bibliographies listing recommended titles for school and public libraries and the average age for titles listed was calculated. The results are given in Table 1. In writing a report, these figures could be used as standards and reported with the figure computed for a specific collection. However, these retrospective bibliographies include very few titles that are out of print, and list items that were available when the bibliography went to press. This policy can result in an average collection age that is younger than necessary, since some useful and formerly recommended titles were out of print when the bibliography was compiled.

COLLECTION USE

Another way of evaluating the collection is by considering its use or potential use. The procedure given below will indicate circulation

Copyright Date	Number of Books	Last Two Digits	Product
1992			
1991			
1990			
1989			
1988			
1987			
1986			
1985			
1984			
1983			
1982			
1981			
1980			
1979			
1978			
1977			
1976			
1975			
1974			
1973			
1972			
1971			

Total products _____

Number of books in sample _____

Average copyright date _____

Figure 6. Average Collection Age Calculation Form

Table 1. Average Age in Years of Materials in Standard Bibliographies[e]

Source	All Items	Fiction	Nonfiction	Space	Vocational Guidance
Children's Catalog[a]	12.90	13.5	12.68	5.91	6
Junior High School Library Catalog[b]	11.45	12.09	11.30	8.59	9.30
Senior High School Library Catalog[c]	14.13	25.08	12.48	8.2	6.74
Elementary School Library Collection[d]	11.0 Total Books 10.3 Total AV 13.7	13.4	9.3	7.3	10.3

[a] *Children's Catalog*, 15th ed. (New York: Wilson Company, 1986).
[b] *Junior High School Library Catalog*, 5th ed. (New York: Wilson, 1985).
[c] *Senior High School Library Catalog*, 13th ed. (New York: Wilson, 1987).
[d] *Elementary School Library Collection: A Guide to Books and Other Media— Phases 1, 2, 3*, 16th ed. (Newark, N.J.: Bro-Dart, 1988).
[e] Average ages calculated using 1990 as the current year.

patterns for the collection. This information can be especially useful for weeding.

1. Sort the sample cards according to the last due date.
2. In Figure 7, fill in the first blank to show the number of titles that falls into each category.
3. Multiply the number in the first blank by 100. Then divide the result by the number of titles in the sample. Enter the result in the second blank. For example, if a sample of 200 includes 6 titles that circulated during the last month, the percent is (6 × 100) ÷ 200 or 3 percent.
4. Numbers of titles or percents can be added directly in order to combine and compare titles in different parts of the collection, such as to find the the percent of the collection that has not circulated in the last year.

It is possible to divide the sample into fiction and nonfiction titles and then follow the procedure given above. The data would allow comparisons to be made between circulation of fiction and nonfiction titles.

Last Due Date	Number of Titles	Percent
< 1 month	_____	_____
1 mo – < 2 mo	_____	_____
2 mo – < 3 mo	_____	_____
3 mo – < 4 mo	_____	_____
4 mo – < 5 mo	_____	_____
5 mo – < 6 mo	_____	_____
6 mo – < 1 yr	_____	_____
1 yr – < 2 yr	_____	_____
2 yr – < 3 yr	_____	_____
3 yr – < 4 yr	_____	_____
4 yr – < 5 yr	_____	_____
5 yr – < 6 yr	_____	_____
6 yr – < 7 yr	_____	_____
7 yr – < 8 yr	_____	_____
8 yr – < 9 yr	_____	_____
9 yr – < 10 yr	_____	_____
10 or more yr	_____	_____

("<" means "less than")

1. Fill in the number of titles which fall into each category. It is easier if you sort the index cards of the sample into piles first.
2. To calculate percent:

$$\frac{(\text{number of titles in the category}) \times 100}{\text{number of titles in the sample}}$$

3. It is possible to add numbers of titles or percents directly in order to combine and compare categories.

Figure 7. Collection Use Chart

This procedure requires the last due date for all titles in the sample. Not all circulation systems keep date-due information, either in the materials or on file. If the last date due is not available, but information about circulating titles is needed, it is possible to use the circulation file. The entire set of materials checked out may be used, or a sample may be taken. Then, the same types of calculations done for the collection sample, such as average age, should be calculated for the circulation sample. Then the two sets of figures can be compared to identify similarities or major differences. Inferential statistics must be used to identify significant differences.

COMPARISON TO STANDARD BIBLIOGRAPHIES

One method of qualitative collection evaluation is to compare the collection to a standard list of recommended materials. The *Elementary School Library Collection, Children's Catalog, Junior High School Library Catalog,* and *Senior High School Library Catalog* can be used for this purpose. It is better to use the most recent editions of these titles. Select the source or sources most appropriate for the collection being analyzed.

Standard retrospective bibliographies can be very useful. They can suggest appropriate titles for school library media collections. They can help in building or evaluating the collection. They represent the collective, professional opinion of knowledgeable librarians or media specialists about which titles could be appropriate for a school library collection.

At the same time, the retrospective bibliographies are generic. That is, the titles suggested are intended for elementary, middle or high schools any place in the United States. Because of this broad focus, titles pertinent to an individual school, school district or other local area may be overlooked. Also, these standard lists can be dated, and new titles, published after the lists are printed, cannot be included. A school library media specialist or librarian must be aware of the specific needs of administrators, teachers and students in his own community or school. Then professional judgment, developed through academic training and personal experience, should be applied to collection development. Each media collection or children's collection should be tailored to meet the needs of its school or community. Follow the steps below to estimate the percent of the collection included in the list of recommended materials.

1. Check the sample titles against the list in the standard source.
2. Separate the sample titles into categories.

Source _____

Dewey Class	Number in Sample	Number Found in Source	Percent Found in Source
000s	_____	_____	_____
100s	_____	_____	_____
200s	_____	_____	_____
300s	_____	_____	_____
400s	_____	_____	_____
500s	_____	_____	_____
600s	_____	_____	_____
700s	_____	_____	_____
800s	_____	_____	_____
900s	_____	_____	_____
Biography	_____	_____	_____
Fiction	_____	_____	_____
Easy Books	_____	_____	_____
Short story	_____	_____	_____
Reference	_____	_____	_____

Total number of titles found _____

Percent of total titles found _____

To calculate percent:
1. Multiply by 100 the number of titles in a category found in the source (center column).
2. Divide the result by the number of sample titles in that category (first column).
3. Enter the result in the third column.

Figure 8. Standard Sources Comparison Form

3. For each line in Figure 8, fill in the first blank (number of sample titles in that category) and the next blank (number of these titles found in the standard source).
4. Using the procedure at the bottom of Figure 8, calculate the percent of titles found in each category. For example, if a

sample included 7 books of short stories, and 2 of these were in the source, the percent is $(2 \times 100) \div 7$ or 29 percent.

5. To calculate the overall percent of titles found in the standard source, multiply the number of titles found in the standard source by 100, and divide by the total number in the sample. For example, if a sample of 200 included 84 that were in the standard source, the percent is $(84 \times 100) \div 200$ or 42 percent.

This procedure may be used for portions of the collection, such as reference titles, audiovisual materials, or periodicals. If the portion of the collection to be evaluated is large, the sample titles that fall into that category may be used. If the number of titles is more limited, e.g., periodicals, all titles in that category may be checked. Figure 9 includes three possible categories, and gives directions for calculating the percentage of titles found in the standard source. A selected list of standard sources appears in the appendixes.

COMPARISON TO TEXTBOOKS OR PERIODICAL INDEXES

In schools it might be beneficial to check the collection to see how many titles are available from the bibliographies listed in textbooks being used in the curriculum. In this case, check the textbook bibliography against the card catalog and determine how many of the recommended titles are in the library collection. (If the sample is checked against the textbook, the results indicate what percent of the total collection is recommended in the text, not what percent of the recommended titles are in the collection.) Figure 10 suggests a form and a procedure for determining the percentage of titles available.

This same procedure can be used to evaluate how well a periodical collection is supported by the periodical index in the school. Use the list of magazines indexed in the reference source as the total number of titles listed. The media center's subscription list is checked against the titles indexed. Again, Figure 10 can be used to calculate the percentage.

In order to document specific areas in the collection that need improvement, it is possible to record teacher requests for curricular materials that the media center is unable to fill. A suggested form is given in Figure 11. At the end of a semester these record sheets could be summarized into one report for (see Figure 18) and included in a report to the principal. This would summarize total numbers only. It may be beneficial to separate the data by Dewey classes to help identify some specific areas where additional materials are needed. For comparison, or to stress positive aspects of

A. Reference Collection

Source Title _____

    a. Number of reference books in sample   _____

    b. Number of these titles found in source   _____

    c. Percent of titles found in source   _____

$$\frac{b \times 100}{a}$$

B. Magazine or Periodical Collection

Source Title _____

    a. Number of magazines in collection   _____

    b. Number of magazines found in source   _____

    c. Percent of magazines found in source   _____

$$\frac{b \times 100}{a}$$

C. Audiovisual Materials

Source Title _____

    a. Number of AV items in sample   _____

    b. Number of AV items found in source   _____

    c. Percent of AV items found in source   _____

$$\frac{b \times 100}{a}$$

Figure 9. Comparison to Specialized Sources

media center service, the same technique could be used to record requests successfully filled.

EVALUATION OF LIMITED AREA

It can have considerable impact sometimes if a more limited area of the collection is identified, data are collected, and calculations are done. Care should be taken to select areas which have changed

Text or Index used _____

    a. Number of titles listed in text or index   _____

    b. Number of titles found in collection   _____

    c. Percent of titles found in collection   _____

$$\frac{b \times 100}{a}$$

Figure 10. Comparison to School Textbook/Periodicals Index

Teacher's name _____

Curricular area _____

Material needed _____

    _____

    _____

Reason unable to supply or slow to obtain material

_____

_____

Will this unit of study be repeated, and the material needed again at a later date?

    _____ yes

    _____ probably

    _____ no

    _____ don't know

Figure 11. Unmet Teacher/Curricular Need

rapidly in recent years or for which having current information is important. Topics such as space exploration or careers can quickly become dated. Sometimes larger areas of the general collection are selected for close evaluation, such as materials with Dewey call numbers in the 500s or 600s. The techniques already discussed for the collection in general can also be used with these limited areas. A suggested summary form is given in Figure 12.

As with overall collection age, average age of space and vocational guidance titles have been calculated for several standard tools. These figures can be used for comparison. (See Table 1.) Be aware of the limitations of these standard sources, as described above.

Figure 13 is a summary sheet. This, or one similar to it, can be used to bring together information in a condensed form. It is often easier for principals, superintendents, and other superiors to digest information presented in this form than it is to study the lengthy calculations performed to arrive at the final figures. The appendix gives citations to sources for national statistics relevant to school libraries, such as average budgeted materials costs. Such data could be used to support and strengthen conclusions arrived at in analysis of an individual collection.

Estimating Update Costs and Benefits

After a summary sheet like Figure 13 has been prepared, it may be necessary to estimate how much it would cost to update the collection. While a precise answer can be difficult to calculate, there are several ways to estimate the cost. Collection age, ability to satisfy teacher requests, or the percent of the collection listed in

---

Special area of study _____

Total number of items included _____

Average age (see Figure 6) _____

Amount of use (see Figure 7) _____

Standard source used for comparison

Number of items found _____

Percent of items found (see Figure 8) _____

Figure 12. Limited Areas for Evaluation

1. School name _____

2. Number of students in school _____

3. Annual media center budget _____
   Amount budgeted per pupil _____

4. Number of books in media center _____
   Number of books per pupil _____

5. Growth rate
   Number of titles added last year _____
   Number of titles lost/weeded last year _____
   Number of AV items added last year _____
   Number of AV items lost/weeded last year _____

6. Average collection age _____

7. Collection circulation figures
   Percent used this year _____
   Percent used last year, and not this year _____
   Percent used before last year and not since _____
   Percent not used _____

8. Comparison to standard sources
   Percent found in general source _____
   Percent found in magazine source _____
   Percent found in reference source _____
   Percent found in AV source _____
   Percent of textbook titles found _____

9. Limited area investigated
   Total number of items investigated _____
   Average age _____
   Amount of use _____
   Standard source used _____
   Percent found in standard source _____

10. Number of unmet teacher or curriculum requests _____
School Media Specialist _____

Figure 13. Summary Sheet—Collection Evaluation

the standard selection aids or school textbooks could be identified as the area needing attention. This decision should be based upon the needs of a particular school and the professional judgment of the media specialist or librarian.

COST OF CHANGING THE AVERAGE AGE OF THE COLLECTION

If the average age of the collection is the primary concern, the following procedure will give a rough estimate of the amount of money needed to lower the average age of the collection. The procedure should be followed for one type of media at a time. For example, books only could be considered first, and the process could be repeated for periodicals or audiovisual materials.

1. Using information from Figure 6, fill in the Average Collection Age in the first line of Figure 14. This is the current status of the collection used for comparison. Since nothing is being replaced, there is no cost on this line.
2. Returning to Figure 6, decide how many of the older titles you will remove, and then remove them. For example, you may choose to remove the 20 oldest titles. In that case, the number 20 goes in the first blank on the second line in Figure 14.
3. Return to Figure 6. Add items with recent copyright dates into the figures to replace those removed in Step 2. For example, if 20 older titles were taken out, you may assume that the replacements will have recent dates and, say, add 10 titles to 1989 and 10 titles to 1990. This is an attempt to predict the copyright dates of replacement titles. Then follow the procedure used in Figure 6 to calculate the revised average collection age. Enter this number in the blank under Resulting Average Collection Age for the second calculation.
4. To estimate the amount of money needed to raise the average collection age by this amount, use Figure 15 and follow the steps given below. You are using the sample data for calcula-

	Number of Titles Dropped	Resulting Average Collection Age (From Fig. 6)	Estimated Replacement Cost (From Fig. 15)
First Calculation	None	_____	None
Second Calculation	_____	_____	_____
Third Calculation	_____	_____	_____
Fourth Calculation	_____	_____	_____
Fifth Calculation	_____	_____	_____

Figure 14. Cost to Lower Average Collection Age

	Second Calculation	Third Calculation	Fourth Calculation	Fifth Calculation
a. Number of Titles Dropped from Sample	_____	_____	_____	_____
b. Total Sample Size	_____	_____	_____	_____
c. Quotient $(a \div b)$	_____	_____	_____	_____
d. Total Collection Size	_____	_____	_____	_____
e. Number of Items to Be Replaced $(c \times d)$	_____	_____	_____	_____
f. Average Cost per Item	_____	_____	_____	_____
g. Estimated Replacement Cost $(e \times f)$	_____	_____	_____	_____

Figure 15. Estimated Replacement Cost

tions but need to purchase replacements for the entire collection, not just the sample. So, this procedure is necessary.
   a. Divide the number of titles dropped from the sample (line a) by the sample size (line b). The resulting number (the quotient) should be a decimal (line c).
   b. Assuming the same number of titles will be replaced, multiply the entire collection size (line d) by the quotient from line c. The product (line e) is the approximate number of items to be replaced in the entire collection.
   c. In line f, enter the average cost for replacing an item. This information is available in the *Library and Book Trade Almanac*, formerly the *Bowker Annual*, and sometimes *School Library Journal*.
   d. Multiply the number of items to be replaced (line e) by the average cost per item (line f). The result is the estimated replacement cost (line g).
5. The estimated cost of replacement can now be transferred to the appropriate space in Figure 14.

For purposes of comparison, it may be appropriate to repeat this procedure one or more times. It must be stressed that these figures are only rough estimates, and not accurate predictions. This procedure assumes that if 20 titles are removed, 20 titles will be purchased to replace them. This may not be true, and could interfere with a media specialist's flexibility. Furthermore, the figure used as the average cost per item is also an estimate. Each replacement item purchased will not cost the same. But the actual average item cost should be fairly close to the estimated average cost. In addition, it is difficult to know exactly the copyright dates of items to be purchased. Recent copyright dates are more probable, but some appropriate older items may be available. Although the estimated cost and revised average collection age are only predictions, sometimes even estimated figures can be appropriate and helpful.

EFFECT OF EXPENDITURES ON AVERAGE COLLECTION AGE

This procedure can be performed in reverse to estimate the impact of a certain amount of funds. For example, a principal may wish to know how much the average collection age would increase if $500 were available for library books.

1. The first step is to use Figure 16 to estimate how many sample items would be replaced.
   a. Divide the amount of money available (line a) by the average cost per item (line b). (This information is available in the *Library and Book Trade Almanac*, formerly the *Bowker Annual*.) The result is the approximate number of items to be replaced in the entire collection (line c).
   b. Divide the number of items to be purchased (line c) by the total collection size (line d). The quotient (line e) should be a decimal.

---

a. Amount of Money Available _____

b. Average Cost per Item _____

c. Number of Items to Be Purchased $(a \div b)$ _____

d. Total Collection Size _____

e. Quotient $(c \div d)$ _____

f. Sample Size _____

g. Number of Sample Titles to Be Replaced $(e \times f)$ _____

Figure 16. Estimate of Sample Items to Be Replaced

Amount of Money Available	Number of Sample Titles Dropped (From Figure 16)	Resulting Average Collection Age (From Figure 6)
_____	_____	_____

Figure 17. Effect of Money on Average Collection Age

     c. Multiply the quotient on line e by the sample size (line f) to find the number of *sample* titles that could be replaced with the money available (line g). In cases where a decimal results, round to the nearest whole number. For example, 5.1 becomes 5 titles and 6.7 would be interpreted as 7 titles. Record the results in Figure 17.
2. Returning to Figure 6, subtract the estimated number of items to be replaced from items belonging to the earlier years on the chart. Then add that number of titles to the items belonging to the more recent years. For example, if Figure 16 indicates 10 items may be replaced, remove 10 of the older items. Then add 5 titles in each of two recent years, e.g., 1991 and 1992.
3. Following the procedure given for Figure 6, recalculate the average collection age using these new figures. Enter the results in Figure 17.

This procedure gives only an estimated or predicted change in average collection age. It does not guarantee accurate figures and is subject to the same constraints and concerns discussed for the cost of changing the average age of the collection. However, there are times when this procedure can be helpful. It may be useful to repeat the procedure for various amounts of money.

Satisfying Teacher Requests

The media specialist, principal or school district may be concerned about the ability of the library collection to meet the curricular needs of teachers. Figure 11 is proposed as one way to keep track of teacher requests that the collection cannot supply at the present time. (Figure 18 can be used to summarize data recorded using Figure 11.) It may be beneficial to separate the data by Dewey classes or subject areas to help identify some specific areas where additional materials are needed or to separate by type of material, e.g., reference, periodicals, or audiovisual. For comparison, or to

| Material | Will it be needed again? | | | |
	Yes	Probably	No	Don't Know
Books	_____	_____	_____	_____
Audiovisual Items	_____	_____	_____	_____
Periodicals	_____	_____	_____	_____
Reference Materials	_____	_____	_____	_____

Figure 18. Number of Unmet Teacher/Curricular Needs

stress positive aspects of media center service, the same report could be used to record requests successfully filled.

To estimate the cost of improving the collection's ability to satisfy teacher's needs, use Figure 19 and the following procedure.

1. Decide which items will be purchased. This could be determined according to subject (e.g., science), type of material (e.g., books), or a combination of both (e.g., science books). It may be appropriate to consider whether or not the material will be needed next semester or next year and count only items that probably will be used again. The media specialist must use her knowledge of the curriculum and personal experience to determine which items to include. Once the decision has been made, the type of title, such as science books, is to be written in the first column of Figure 19. The number of items proposed for purchase belongs in the second column.
2. Using the *Library and Book Trade Almanac*, formerly the *Bowker Annual* or some other source, enter the average cost per item in the third column.

Item	Number of Items to Purchase	Average Cost Per Item*	Estimated Cost
_____	_____	_____	_____
_____	_____	_____	_____
_____	_____	_____	_____

*This information can be obtained from the *Library and Book Trade Almanac*, formerly the *Bowker Annual*.

Figure 19. Estimated Cost of Meeting Teacher Needs

3. Multiply the number of items to purchase by the average cost per item to estimate the cost of purchasing these items.

The number calculated estimates the cost of purchasing all of the identified items. Because there is no sampling involved in this procedure, the number of items and the resulting estimated cost are directly related. For example, if only half of the identified items are purchased, the corresponding estimated cost will be half as large. If 10 items would cost $90, then 5 items would cost $45. That is, if one is changed by multiplication or division, the effect on the other figure can be determined by multiplying or dividing it in the same way.

It must be remembered that the cost calculated is an estimate. The items purchased will not all cost the same, but the actual average should approximate the average from the *Library and Book Trade Almanac*. Probably not all the items requested by the teachers will be available for purchase, and the teachers will have new requests next year. But this procedure should estimate some of the costs to improve the ability of the collection to meet teacher's curricular needs.

Conclusion

In this chapter you have been given a variety of techniques for analyzing the data collected in your sample. Once you have clarified your objectives, it is simply a matter of utilizing the data to your advantage.

THREE

Weeding

What Is Weeding?

WEEDING IS AN essential but often overlooked aspect of collection development. It is sometimes thought of as selection in reverse, because it removes materials from the collection when they are no longer useful. This process has been described as retirement, pruning, reverse selection, deselection, relegation, and discarding.[1] However because most of the terms have negative connotations, it is sometimes difficult to convince administrators that this is an important function, especially since school library collection evaluations for accreditation are most often based on the total number of books. Perhaps we need a more positive term to describe this process, such as collection enhancement or collection re-evaluation.

No matter what we call it, a good working definition is important. One such definition is "the practice of discarding or transferring to storage excess copies, rarely used books and materials no longer of use."[2] Stueart makes the point that weeding and discarding are sometimes used interchangeably, but in fact are not synonymous.[3] According to the definition given, storage is an optional aspect of weeding. Storing enables the library to retain the material but at a second level of access usually not open to the public.[4]

Now that we have a working definition, it is time to take the next step. The professional literature about weeding stresses the importance of planning so that decisions are based on facts, not whims or hunches. Before any program is implemented, the library's goals need to be re-evaluated to ensure that the materials being weeded will be those that are no longer relevant to the library's collection.

Evaluation of Policy and Goals

The new standards for school library media centers as set forth in *Information Power* address the importance of policy formulation in collection development. "All schools must have a collection development plan that addresses their collection needs and includes such specific steps as school and community analysis, policy development, selection, acquisition, weeding, and evaluation."[5] Note that weeding is seen here as an important aspect of collection development. Selection of materials and weeding are similar activities; they require the same kinds of decision making. The key concepts in collection development, just as in collection analysis, are management and planning.

In establishing a weeding program, Stueart cautions, "to reduce the hazards implicit in weeding, three essential steps should be included in the initial planning process: (1) analysis of needs, (2) analysis of options, and (3) determination of what is feasible."[6] His article presents a comprehensive overview of the topic and addresses many of the most common concerns about the process, such as reasons for weeding, i.e., redundancy in the collection, shifts in goals and emphases of the library, physical deterioration or obsolescence of materials, and the need for space. He also discusses several points that need to be considered in developing a weeding strategy, such as cost, politics, the availability of storage, and cooperative agreements. To avoid problems, there is much to consider, such as checking to see if there are any local constraints, regulations, or statutes that might affect your weeding program or laws that might prohibit the sale of books.

Phyllis Van Orden lists the following points to consider in developing a policy for re-evaluating items in your collections to determine which items should be repaired, replaced or removed from the collection.[7]

1. What will happen if someone needs the materials that have been removed?
2. How can we provide a replacement policy to assure that a decrease in numbers of items held will not lead to a budget cut?
3. What will the source of funding be for the cost of the reevaluation, if additional personnel are needed?
4. How will the transfer or disposal of materials and equipment be handled?

By considering these and other factors, you can form or review your collection development policies and goals. After a policy is in place, you must translate it into action. Most of us are not able to go through our collections from one end to the other, so it is useful to consider other strategies. Oftentimes we have space problems in a specific area of our collection or subjects have been added to or deleted from the curriculum. Then it is useful to identify priorities or areas of immediate need to establish a schedule for weeding. It is important to consider what is feasible with the staff available, the structure of the weeding program, and the establishment of a timetable. We need to decide whether or not we will opt for continuous weeding as materials are returned, or intermittent weeding throughout the year, or occasional weeding as part of a day or for a whole day.[8] Unless we make time for it, it will not get done.

Barriers to Weeding

In weeding, the same steps that placed materials on the shelves are performed in reverse. It is a time-consuming effort. Our professional literature is filled with reasons, rationalizations and excuses for why we do not weed our collections. The following are the reasons most frequently cited.

1. I am too busy—I have no time to weed. We would find the time if we knew how much it costs us to house a dead or an obsolete book. (Thirty years ago it was 40 cents per book; twenty years ago, $1.25; four years ago, $5.06.)
2. Books are sacred. We have emotional and intellectual blocks against removing books from a collection. Many of us consider books to be valuable records of our human heritage. Removing them becomes painful.
3. A book might be needed by someone at some time in the future. This is rare. It is much more likely that you will be asked for a book that you never acquired. Few libraries, even the large research libraries, can afford to house a book until sometime in the future when someone shows up to use it. A more realistic approach is to consider cooperation and networking with other libraries. Make agreements about what will be collected and kept by whom.
4. Numbers are considered a criterion of the quality of a library. We are forced to play a numbers game and include obsolete books in the official count. Unfortunately quantity is no indication of quality. A good library is not necessarily a big library.
5. I hate to admit that I made a mistake in selecting this book. So what? Because book selection is not based on scientific formulas or objective measurements, but rather on the librarian's

judgment of books and people, every librarian has probably made some mistakes. There were all sorts of variables at work when that book was selected, i.e., how much money you had, interest in the subject at that time, availability of other titles on the same subject, etc. You can sharpen your judgment by experience and training, but you can never make it infallible.
6. Weeding is just willful destruction of public property. No, it is a very constructive process, as outlined in the next section.

In Defense Of Weeding

Weeding is one aspect of collection development, and a natural follow-up to collection evaluation. Weeding occurs when materials no longer appropriate for a collection are removed from it. While many librarians and media specialists acknowledge the need for and value of weeding, parents, teachers and administrators do not always understand. The following reasons for weeding can both stimulate the professional's own thinking and be used to explain weeding to others.

Weeding can remove materials which are outdated or superseded. For example, a book that indicates the first step in growing pop-corn is to hitch the horse to the plow would be a candidate for removal. Chances are extremely good that the information it contains is badly outdated.

Information in some materials may be inaccurate or dangerous, perpetuate stereotypes or somehow contain misinformation. Too frequently, biographies for children have errors, as Moore shows clearly in her article. Some science-fair books instruct children to build a volcano using matches instead of baking soda and vine-gar. Chemistry books may advocate dangerous experiments. Some books do stereotype minorities, women, the aged, or other groups in ways that are clearly inappropriate. The media specialist or librarian can justify removing these materials.

Some of the materials in a library collection, either through normal use or borrower carelessness, become damaged. They may be dropped in a mud puddle, chewed by the dog, or colored by helpful hands. Pages may be torn or missing; the binding may no longer hold the book together; the cover may fall off. The projector may mangle a filmstrip; a record may become badly scratched; a micro-computer disk may be bent. The types and causes of damage are many and varied. Some items can be repaired. Others may need to be weeded.

Library users and their needs change. Therefore, a library collection must also change if it is to continue to meet the needs of its users. This can be done by purchasing new items. But it is also helpful to remove items which are no longer pertinent.

As materials are removed from the collection, there can be a number of positive outcomes. For example, weeding can relieve overcrowding and make for new acquisitions. Access to the remaining materials can be greatly improved because it is easier to find an item if there are fewer materials to search. Often, the weeded collection will become more physically attractive. As its appearance improves, users may begin to have more respect for items in the collection, and therefore treat them more carefully.

The number of volumes in a collection, by itself, is not a good indicator of its quality. Other factors, such as age, and currency and accuracy of the content of items in the collection must be considered. At the same time, standards and regulations may rely on collection size to indicate quality. Weeding the collection helps decrease reliance on numbers alone, and can improve the overall collection by removing substandard items.

Weeding can be cost-effective. There are continuing costs associated with maintaining a library media center collection. Besides the ordinary costs of heating, cooling, and so forth, there are specific activities associated with the collection. Shelves must be read, to keep materials in the proper order. Items must be dusted and kept clean. All materials should be inventoried regularly. The card catalog and shelflist must be maintained. It is a drain on library resources to perform these activities for items which no longer belong in the collection.

As technology improves and becomes more affordable, more and more libraries are converting to online catalogs and circulation systems. It is not efficient to spend time and money entering materials into the new system when those items no longer belong in the collection. Therefore, weeding should be done before automating the library or media center.

General Guidelines for Weeding

Given that weeding is an integral part of collection development, decisions on whether to retain or remove an item must be made on an individual basis. There is no easy-to-follow rule or set of rules to use in making each decision. Instead, each librarian or media specialist must apply professional judgment and a thorough knowledge of the user community when weeding the collection. However, there are some general guidelines which may be helpful.

The physical condition of an item may be reason for removal. It may be so battered, torn, dirty or damaged that it is not worth the time and effort needed to recondition it. Small print, missing pages or chewed-up frames on a filmstrip can also indicate removal.

Duplicate copies can be justified for items that are in great demand. As use declines, the extra copies can become candidates for weeding. Other changes in user needs, such as curriculum revisions, can result in decreased use of some items in the collection. If Latin has not been taught in a school for the last twenty years, does its media center still need thirty titles in Latin?

With time, the utility of some items decreases, and it may be appropriate to remove them from the collection. It is reasonable to question the value of a set of encyclopedias published in 1953. Published guidelines, such as those in Van Orden's book, are available, which suggest appropriate ages or circulation data for weeding different subject areas and various types of materials. For other items, content may be superseded by newer editions or recent developments, in addition to the general age guidelines. If a new edition is published, does the collection really need two earlier editions also? There are some fields, such as space flight, which change very rapidly. Older titles in these areas should be checked for obsolescence, and removed when they become dated.

There are materials in any library media center collection that do not belong there. Some items are not being used, either in or out of the library. The library users may have changed. If the media center originally served kindergarten through sixth grade, but now the users are primary-grade children, then many books on the fifth- and sixth-grade reading levels may no longer be needed. There may be unsolicited gifts in the collection that don't meet the criteria in the selection policy. Some items may have been acquired through mistakes in selection. Any materials that are inappropriate for a particular collection are candidates for removal.

For some items, initial purchase is justified. These include the local newspapers and magazines of special interest to users. But if these are not indexed, there is little need to keep many back issues. Without access, information in these items is almost impossible to locate. So it is better to use available storage for magazines, newspapers and other items where it is possible to find specific articles or other contents easily.

General Guidelines for Retention

The comments given above are intended as general guidelines only. The professional judgment of the librarian or media specialist must be used throughout the entire procedure. When a decision is made about removing an item, that decision may be guided by the rules of thumb given here. But the librarian's personal experience, knowledge, and familiarity with the users are also vitally important.

Just as there are some materials that should be weeded, there are some items that should be retained in a collection, such as items that are still being used by a particular user or user group. One book, for instance, may be especially adept at introducing children to an idea or stimulating discussion. That title is important to the adults who continue to use it with children. When useful items are identified, and if they are out of print or otherwise unavailable, they probably should not be discarded. In this case, even older or worn titles may need to be retained.

It is important to be aware of the overall balance of the collection. If removing materials would impair collection coverage in a particular subject area, it may be better to retain the items. Sometimes it is possible to have certain titles rebound. Other repairs may help extend the life of certain materials.

In general, the classics have a place in children's collections. Unless a newer, more attractive edition is available, those titles should be kept. Also, within the bounds of professional judgment, it may be valuable to retain items listed in a current edition of a standard bibliography for a particular library.

Some materials are of special interest to an individual library. These may include titles about local or state history or peripheral items pertinent to individuals or groups in the community. Local publications, such as school yearbooks, can be of interest. These items can be difficult or impossible to replace, and are often of continuing interest or importance. They should be retained in the collection, unless they are available elsewhere in the community. (For example, newspapers often keep their own backfiles of publications.)

Some items may be of interest to a particular library. For instance, a prominent local author may present autographed copies of his books to the library. Titles purchased with memorial funds may fall into this category. There may be an occasional rare book. These items may need to be retained. If such an item is identified it may be helpful to prominently stamp it, "Do not discard."

There are no ironclad rules for weeding. There are only general guidelines to help the librarian or media specialist apply professional judgment.

How to Discard Library Materials

Once you have actually removed items from your collection, you are faced with having to get rid of them. This can sometimes be a ticklish situation, and horror stories abound concerning discarded items that return to haunt their original owners. You need to develop a plan based on your own situation. The following list of methods that have been tried comes from Iowa's Department of Public Instruction:[9]

1. Bag and tag for destruction.
2. Put a few in each waste basket every day.
3. Take them to the dump.
4. Take them to another community's dump.
5. Tear or break them up and put them in a waste basket.
6. Offer them to a charity book sale–many such groups now sell magazines, records, etc. as well as books.
7. Have a white elephant sale.
8. Offer other libraries in the community an opportunity to select anything they can use.
9. Box and send them to the superintendent.
10. Store them until they are forgotten.

The same publication offers some important points to consider when selecting a method.[10]

1. The method(s) selected should be in harmony with school policy.
2. The school district selection policy should specifically assign responsibility for discarding library materials and equipment to the library media specialists, including responsibility to determine intrinsic worth.
3. The school district should use established depreciation tables for library materials and equipment. Such tables also help justify discarding materials and equipment purchased with general funds.
4. All items not destroyed should have all identifying marks removed or be clearly marked as discarded.
5. Library materials in classrooms need to be weeded too. The classroom should not become a dump. If older items such as

sets of encyclopedias are placed in the classrooms they should be discarded after a specified time, such as ten years.

6. If major weeding is to be done, the school and community should be prepared and advised that regular weeding in the future will be at a more sedate pace.

The methods outlined are for your consideration. Each situation is unique. As professionals, you will be able to plan and implement the most effective weeding program for your library.

Notes

1. Robert D. Stueart, "Weeding of Library Materials—Politics and Policies" in *Collection Management* (Summer 1985), 48.

2. Edward G. Evans, *Developing Library and Information Center Collections*, 2d ed. (Littleton, Colo.: Libraries Unlimited, 1987), p. 291.

3. Stueart, p. 48.

4. Evans, p. 292.

5. American Association of School Librarians and Association for Educational Communications and Technology, *Information Power* (Chicago: American Library Association; Washington, D.C.: Association for Educational Communication and Technology, 1988), p. 73.

6. Stueart, p. 48.

7. Phyllis J. Van Orden, *The Collection Program in Schools* (Englewood, Colo.: Libraries Unlimited, 1988), p. 242.

8. Van Orden, p. 243.

9. Betty Jo Buckingham, *Weeding the Library Media Center Collections*. (Des Moines: State of Iowa, Department of Public Instruction, 1984), p. 15.

10. Buckingham, p. 15.

Selected Readings

Calgary Board of Education, Educational Media Team. "Weeding the School Library Media Collection." *School Library Media Quarterly* (Fall 1984): 419-24.
    The document used in the Calgary (Alberta, Canada) public schools to guide weeding in the system media centers to strengthen collections.

Carter, Mary D., and Wallace J. Bonk. "How–and Where–to Weed." *Library Journal* (January 15, 1960): 198–200.
    General discussion of why weeding doesn't occur, reasons to do it, and some general guidelines for categories of books.

Erlich, Mary. "Do Not Discard." *The U*N*A*B*A*S*H*E*D Librarian* (Number 16): 9–10:
    Explains philosophy and technique for permanently identifying items that are *not* to be weeded from the collection.

Evans, Edward G: *Developing Library Collections*. Littleton, Colo.: Libraries Unlimited, 1979.
    Set in the context of collection development, this chapter gives a good overview of the entire topic of weeding.
Gordon, Anitra. "Weeding: Keeping Up with the Information Explosion." *School Library Journal* (September 1983): 45–46.
    Stresses the need to involve teachers in the weeding process, and has a nice discussion of some general guidelines for weeding.
Katz, William A. *Collection Development: The Selection of Materials for Libraries*. New York: Holt, Rinehart and Winston, 1980.
    Part of a book on collection development, weeding is shown to be as important as selection. Also, there are separate sections on weeding periodicals and gifts.
McGaw, Howard F. "Policies and Practices in Discarding." *Library Trends* 4 (1956): 269–81.
    A general discussion of weeding and the justification for the process. Also gives some general guidelines for weeding.
Manning, Pat and Alan R. Newman. "Safety Isn't Always First: A Disturbing Look at Chemistry Books." *School Library Journal* (October 1986): 99–102.
    Carefully details some specific dangers to look for in chemistry books, such as heating carbon tetrachloride.
Miller, J. Wesley: "Throwing Out Belles Lettres with the Bathwater." *American Libraries* (June 1984): 384–85.
    Eloquently makes the point that librarians need to be familiar with their community and collections to avoid weeding materials that should be retained.
Moore, Ann W. "A Question of Accuracy: Errors in Children's Biographies." *School Library Journal* (February 1985): 34–35.
    Identifies specific examples of errors that fall into three categories–mistakes on items (e.g., dates) that could be easily checked; errors caused by attempts to simplify content; and "patently false, incorrect information."
Reed-Scott, Jutta. "Implementation and Evaluation of a Weeding Program." *Collection Management* (Summer 1985): 59–67.
    A successful weeding program requires detailed planning and careful development of criteria.
Rush, Betsy. "Weeding vs. Censorship: Treading a Fine Line." *School Library Journal* (November 1974): 42–43.
    Discusses the re-evaluation process and techniques used in a public library to identify dated young adult fiction.
Segal, Joseph P. *Evaluating and Weeding Collections in Small and Medium-sized Public Libraries–the CREW Method*. Chicago: American Library Association, 1976.
    An in-depth discussion of weeding, with philosophy, guidelines and suggested techniques. Designed as a handbook.
Stueart, Robert D. "Weeding of Library Materials–Politics and Policies." *Collection Management* (Summer 1985): 47–58.
    An overview of the weeding process is presented with a review of its nature, purpose, and proper functioning.

Van Orden, Phyllis J. *The Collection Program in Schools: Concepts, Practices and Information Sources*. Englewood, Colo.: Libraries Unlimited, 1988.
The section on weeding is directed at school media centers and has a nice discussion of reasons why weeding is avoided.
Wezeman, Frederick: "Psychological Barriers to Weeding." *ALA Bulletin* (September 1958): 637–39.
A brief discussion of the psychological barriers to weeding and why librarians need to overcome those barriers.

FOUR

Automation and Your Library Collection

AUTOMATION IS COMING to school library media centers. If some or all of your media center operations are not already automated, computers will probably be coming in the future. When it is time to automate, it is very important to be prepared and to remember that the changes can affect all aspects of media center services and operations. In planning, be sure to consider facilities, costs, staff training, media and cataloging standards, hardware and software, whether the systems can be upgraded, and emerging technologies. Planning for automation should start with appointing a committee, reading about both the technologies and experiences some libraries have had with them, and visiting and consulting with other knowledgeable professionals. Information available in the library literature can help in planning for and implementing automation.

When the decision has been made to automate the circulation system or the card catalog, the collection itself becomes one focus of attention. Information in the shelflist must be converted into a machine-readable database available to the computer. Because the system will use this information to operate, it must be accurate. This means that the shelflist itself must be correct and current *before* the information is transferred to the computer.

Verification of the Shelflist

For each item, the shelflist should list the correct author, title, publisher, date, and local Dewey decimal call number. The systems allow at least two or three subject headings per title. (One program, Mandarin, allows more than sixty.) Most computer vendors use Library of Congress subject headings, instead of Sears. And the ISBN (International Standard Book Number) or LCCN (Library of Congress Card Number) for each book is the identification code used to enter the information in the database.

When the collection is being prepared for automation, the shelflist must be verified in the following areas:

1. Check to see that the information on the cards is correct and readable. Each shelflist card should represent one unique title.
2. Verify that each item has not been withdrawn and is not missing.
3. Decide whether or not items need to be weeded.
4. The local Dewey numbers should be consistent, e.g., numbers within the same classification must be carried out to the same number of places past the decimal. Follow the AACR2 cataloging code. All biography should be assigned the same numbers, not scattered among B, 92, and 921.
5. The ISBN or LCCN must be given for each title.
6. The number of copies, volumes, or editions should be clearly and readily readable.
7. If the system allows for special categories (e.g., read-aloud books), be sure the correct codes are shown on the shelflist cards.

Estimating Time Required for Verification

The random sample drawn for earlier collection analysis can be used to estimate the amount of work required to prepare the collection for automation. Use Figure 20 and the following procedure.

a. Sample time   _____

b. Sample size   _____

c. Total collection size   _____

d. Quotient (line c ÷ line b)   _____

e. Product or estimated time

   (line d × line a)   _____

Figure 20. Estimating from Sample Times to Entire Collection

1. Verify the shelflist using the steps given above. Record the time it takes for each step, several steps at once, or the entire operation.
2. Once you know how long it takes to verify or to partially verify the sample, the following procedures will estimate the time needed to do that operation for the entire shelflist:
   a. Enter the time (in minutes) taken to complete the operation on line a.
   b. Enter the sample size on line b.
   c. Enter the total collection size on line c.
   d. Divide the total collection size by the sample size. The resulting number, or quotient, is to be entered on line d.
   e. Multiply the result of step d, or the quotient, by the time taken to work on the sample from line a. The result is the estimated time needed to perform the timed-job for the entire shelflist.

If, for example, your sample of 200 cards was drawn from a shelflist of 3,891, your quotient would be 19.04. If you found that the time required to do one operation on the sample was 240 minutes, then 240 × 19.04 or 4,569.6 minutes (about 76 hours) may be needed to do the operation on the entire shelflist.

In addition to using the sample from your library to estimate the time needed to prepare your shelflist for automation, time estimates are available in *Media Center Automation. Circulation: The Way to Go* (or the corresponding *School Library Journal* article by Holloway). According to these sources, it took one person sixty minutes or two people forty minutes to verify a shelf of fifty books. Information from this source could be used to support or replace calculations based on the sample drawn from your collection.

Database Creation

After the shelflist has been checked and the information on the cards is correct, the database can be created. That is, the information on the shelflist cards can be transferred to the computer. This can be done by typing into the computer the information on each card. Or it is possible to use the ISBN or LCCN to have the computer itself read and transfer the bibliographic information from a set of titles already available in the computer. (This can work quite well, but it is still necessary to type in some titles.) Taken together, all of the pieces of information about the materials in the library collection and available to the computer in a form it can manipulate become the database for the library. The computer uses this information for searching for particular titles, books by an author, or materials on a requested subject.

When the shelflist is entered into a database, the work can be done in one of three ways. The vendor can do all of the work, the school library media specialist and other local people can enter everything, or some input can be done locally and some by the vendor. More information on the advantages, disadvantages, and costs of each can be found in the Murphy article and in *Media Center Automation. Circulation: The Way to Go.* It is advisable to carefully consider and compare the options. It may be helpful to create a chart showing estimated times, costs, advantages and disadvantages of each. Be sure to include the labor costs of local data entry, and remember that other services may be affected if staff time is spent entering data.

It is also important to carefully and thoroughly weed the collection before automation is performed. This advice is repeated and repeatedly emphasized in the library literature. Materials that are outdated, worn, or unused will not be transformed just because they are listed in the computer database. Although improved access to the content of some titles, such as collective biographies, may increase their use, this is not true of most materials. Furthermore, it costs money for each title that is entered into the database. Estimated costs for data entry done by vendors range from $0.23 to $1 per record, so weeding before automating is cost-effective.

Estimating the Number of Titles to Be Weeded

The random sample drawn for collection analysis may be used to estimate how many titles should be weeded from the collection. Follow the same basic procedure discussed earlier to estimate the time needed to verify the shelflist (see Figure 21).

---

a. Number of sample titles to be weeded   _____

b. Sample size   _____

c. Total collection size   _____

d. Quotient (line a ÷ line b)   _____

e. Product or number of books to be weeded

    (line d × line c)   _____

Figure 21. Estimated Number of Titles or Volumes to Be Weeded

1. Using the criteria for weeding discussed earlier, determine how many of the sample items should be weeded. (You may wish to divide these into first candidates for weeding, then second candidates, or rank them in some way.) The resulting number should be entered on line a.
2. Then, follow these steps:
    a. Enter sample size on line b.
    b. Enter the total collection size on line c.
    c. Divide the number of titles weeded (line a) by the sample size (line b). Enter the result, or quotient, on line d.
    d. Multiply the quotient (line d) by the total collection size (line c). The resulting product is the estimated total number of items to be weeded from the collection.

For example, if 34 items were weeded from the sample of 200, the quotient is .17. If the total collection size is 3,500, about 595 books may need to be weeded (i.e., $.17 \times 3,500 = 595$).

If items to be weeded were divided into subgroups such as first and second priority for weeding (Step 1), repeat Step 2 for each subgroup.

The result will be an estimate of the number of volumes that could be removed from the collection. Multiplying this figure by the estimated cost per title for entering the title into the automated system will estimate the savings to be gained by first weeding the collection. The Murphy article lists some estimated costs per title for data entry.

Considerations in System Selection

When purchasing an automated system, some collection data can help determine which system may be best. These figures are the following:

the total size of the collection, including materials in all formats

the number of titles added to or removed from the collection annually

which items in the school library media center will be entered into the database, which won't be entered, and why

the number of weekly circulating titles and overdues (especially important for circulation systems)

any special features desired (e.g., multiple subject headings or ability to generate bibliographies)

This information can help when hardware and software are being considered. After collection size and use figures are available, it is easier to identify programs or machines which can handle the workload of your media center. This information can help identify special features that may be of interest. For example, can titles or users be readily added or deleted as needed, or must this or can this be done by the vendor? Is the hardware powerful enough to handle a collection this large? This information may also be used to justify requests for automation (e.g., if you find it takes 15 hours a week to write overdues slips).

Finally, it may be important to have a system that will help evaluate both the collection and the services. Consider what the automated systems could do to help with future evaluations using the procedures presented in this book and information about your collection. For example, can the system generate a random sample for you? If not, will it allow you to identify a random sample? (For instance, if the bar codes are assigned serially, do you know the first and last numbers, and can you access an individual title through the bar code?) Can the circulation system keep a record of the last date due for titles that circulate? Can the system calculate average collection age? What information will you need about the collection in the future and can the system help you find it and use it? Cooke's article details one way an automated circulation system helped to identify titles to consider for weeding.

Summary

When planning for automation, the collection itself must be carefully prepared. Preparing the shelflist and weeding are two of the most important and time-consuming steps that precede automation. When purchasing a system, consider the current demand of library operations and what the future demands may be. Careful planning by informed media specialists can help ensure successful automation.

Selected Readings

Champion, Sandra. "Technostress: Technology's Toll." *School Library Journal* (November 1988): 48–57.
    Discusses the emotional and psychological impact of the new technologies on some people.
Cooke, Deborah. "Getting the Most Out of Your Computer Circulation System." *Book Report* (September/October 1989): 11–12.

Describes the author's use of an automated circulation system to help weed fiction.

Grael, Bob. "Sabotage from Within: Pitfalls in Choosing a Circulation System." *Book Report* (September/October 1989): 8–10.

A brief discussion of the problems that result when automation decisions are based on too little knowledge.

Hansen, James O., Jane Kilbe, and Donna Gilliland. *School Library Media Programs: A Resource and Planning Guide for South Dakota Schools.* np, np, 1989.

A complete guide to program operations and planning with sections on collection evaluation, weeding and automation. Includes bibliographies.

Holloway, Mary A. "Media Center Automation: The Way to Go!" *School Library Journal* (August 1988): 41–44.

Based on experiences in automating two North Carolina school circulation systems, this briefly outlines the planning, development and implementation of those systems.

Kemper, Marilyn. "Emerging Technologies: A Roadmap for Librarians:" *School Library Journal* (November 1988): 36–41.

A brief discussion of electronic mail, desk-top publishing, local area networks, and fax, with a strategy for development of new technologies.

Kroll, Carol. "Preparing the Collection for Retrospective Conversion." *School Library Media Quarterly* (Winter 1990): 82–83:

Quick overview of standardization, networking, weeding and inventory as they relate to preparing for automation.

Media Center Automation. Circulation: The Way to Go. Division of Computer Services, Media and Technology Services. North Carolina Department of Public Instruction (Raleigh NC 27603-1712)

A valuable, detailed discussion and guide to the planning for and implementation of automated circulation systems.

Murphy, Catherine. "Questions to Guide Retrospective Conversion Choices for School Library Media Centers." *School Library Media Quarterly* (Winter 1990): 79-81.

A practical list of questions to help librarians in planning for automation. Includes a chart of conversion options and estimated costs.

————. "The Time Is Right to Automate." *School Library Journal* (November 1988):42–47.

A general discussion of things to consider in planning for automation.

Rogers, Jo Ann V. "Mainstreaming Media Center Materials: Adopting AACR2." *School Library Journal* (April 1981): 32–35.

Rogers argues strongly for school library media centers to adhere to cataloging standards.

Skapura, Robert. "A Primer on Automating the Card Catalog." *School Library Media Quarterly* (Winter 1990): 75-78.

Gives reasons for and discussion of the issues about automating the card catalog.

Conclusion

COLLECTION DEVELOPMENT is one of the professional aspects of working as a school library media specialist. The programming and services provided to teachers and students often depend on the media center's collection; therefore, it is important for that collection to be current, well-maintained, and able to meet the needs of its users. One of the more important steps in collection development is evaluating materials. This can help identify strengths and weaknesses of the collection. Equally important, this evaluation can help communicate the strengths and weaknesses to administrators. (In today's competitive world, it is important for school library media specialists to be able to succinctly and numerically present a written justification for budgetary requests.) The first portions of this book have presented one method of collection evaluation that has proven to be successful both for providing information about the collection and justifying funding requests.

Another important, and often underrated, part of collection development is weeding the collection. It is not enough to add newer relevant materials to a media center collection. The older, outdated, or useless items must also be removed. Because there is some tendency to neglect weeding, and because there is some resistance to weeding, this book has dealt with some of the reasons and techniques for removing items from media center collections.

Finally, automation has, is, or will soon be coming to media centers. Because the techniques presented in this book can help plan for automation, and because the collection itself must be considered when automating, the last portion of this book has addressed those issues.

While the procedures presented here may seem time-consuming or intimidating, remember that others have successfully used them to improve media center collections and to improve their funding. You can too!

Standard Sources

The following sources are updated periodically. In order to conduct an effective collection analysis, consult the most recent edition.

Brown, Lucy Gregor. *Core Media Collection for Secondary Schools.* New York: Bowker

—— and Betty McDavid. *Core Media Collection for Elementary Schools.* New York: Bowker

Children's Catalog. New York: H.W. Wilson

Children's Magazine Guide: Subject Index to Children's Magazines. Madison, Wisc.: P.T. Rowland

Elementary School Library Collection: A Guide to Books and Other Media—Phases 1, 2, 3. Ed. by Lois Winkel. Newark, N.J.: Bro-Dart

Junior High School Library Catalog. New York: H.W. Wilson

Peterson, Carol Sue. *Reference Books for Elementary and Junior High School Libraries.* Metuchen, N.J.: Scarecrow

Readers' Guide to Periodical Literature. New York: H.W. Wilson

Richardson, Selma. *Magazines for Children.* Chicago: American Library Association

Senior High School Library Catalog. New York: H.W. Wilson

Wynar, Christine L. *Guide to Reference Books for School Media Centers.* Littleton, Colo.: Libraries Unlimited

Forms

Category	Length
000s	————
100s	————
200s	————
300s	————
400s	————
500s	————
600s	————
700s	————
800s	————
900s	————
Biography	————

Total nonfiction ————————

Fiction	————
Easy Books	————
Short stories	————

Total fiction ————————

Reference	————
Audiovisual	————
Other	————

Total miscellaneous ————————

Total shelflist ————————

Figure 3. Shelflist Measuring Form

Author _____

Title _____

Call No. _____

Copyright Date _____

Listed in Standard Sources:

_____

_____

_____

_____

Last Due Date _____

Figure 4. Possible Format for Sample Card

Dewey Class	Length in cm	Percent
000s	_____	_____
100s	_____	_____
200s	_____	_____
300s	_____	_____
400s	_____	_____
500s	_____	_____
600s	_____	_____
700s	_____	_____
800s	_____	_____
900s	_____	_____
Biography	_____	_____
Fiction	_____	_____
Easy Books	_____	_____
Short stories	_____	_____
Reference	_____	_____
Audiovisual	_____	_____

To calculate the percent for each category:
1. Multiply the number of centimeters in that category times 100.
2. Divide by the total number of centimeters in the shelflist. Use the total shelflist number from Figure 3.
3. Enter the result in the "Percent" column.

Figure 5. Calculating Collection Percentages

Copyright Date	Number of Books	Last Two Digits	Product
1992	_____	_____	_____
1991	_____	_____	_____
1990	_____	_____	_____
1989	_____	_____	_____
1988	_____	_____	_____
1987	_____	_____	_____
1986	_____	_____	_____
1985	_____	_____	_____
1984	_____	_____	_____
1983	_____	_____	_____
1982	_____	_____	_____
1981	_____	_____	_____
1980	_____	_____	_____
1979	_____	_____	_____
1978	_____	_____	_____
1977	_____	_____	_____
1976	_____	_____	_____
1975	_____	_____	_____
1974	_____	_____	_____
1973	_____	_____	_____
1972	_____	_____	_____
1971	_____	_____	_____

Total products _____

Number of books in sample _____

Average copyright date _____

Figure 6. Average Collection Age Calculation Form

Last Due Date	Number of Titles	Percent
< 1 month	_____	_____
1 mo – < 2 mo	_____	_____
2 mo – < 3 mo	_____	_____
3 mo – < 4 mo	_____	_____
4 mo – < 5 mo	_____	_____
5 mo – < 6 mo	_____	_____
6 mo – < 1 yr	_____	_____
1 yr – < 2 yr	_____	_____
2 yr – < 3 yr	_____	_____
3 yr – < 4 yr	_____	_____
4 yr – < 5 yr	_____	_____
5 yr – < 6 yr	_____	_____
6 yr – < 7 yr	_____	_____
7 yr – < 8 yr	_____	_____
8 yr – < 9 yr	_____	_____
9 yr – < 10 yr	_____	_____
10 or more yr	_____	_____

("<" means "less than")

1. Fill in the number of titles which fall into each category. It is easier if you sort the index cards of the sample into piles first.
2. To calculate percent:

$$\frac{(\text{number of titles in the category}) \times 100}{\text{number of titles in the sample}}$$

3. It is possible to add numbers of titles or percents directly in order to combine and compare categories.

Figure 7. Collection Use Chart

Source _____

Dewey Class	Number in Sample	Number Found in Source	Percent Found in Source
000s	_____	_____	_____
100s	_____	_____	_____
200s	_____	_____	_____
300s	_____	_____	_____
400s	_____	_____	_____
500s	_____	_____	_____
600s	_____	_____	_____
700s	_____	_____	_____
800s	_____	_____	_____
900s	_____	_____	_____
Biography	_____	_____	_____
Fiction	_____	_____	_____
Easy Books	_____	_____	_____
Short story	_____	_____	_____
Reference	_____	_____	_____

Total number of titles found   _____

Percent of total titles found   _____

To calculate percent:
1. Multiply by 100 the number of titles in a category found in the source (center column).
2. Divide the result by the number of sample titles in that category (first column).
3. Enter the result in the third column.

Figure 8. Standard Sources Comparison Form

A. Reference Collection

Source Title _____

    a. Number of reference books in sample   _____

    b. Number of these titles found in source   _____

    c. Percent of titles found in source   _____

$$\frac{b \times 100}{a}$$

B. Magazine or Periodical Collection

Source Title _____

    a. Number of magazines in collection   _____

    b. Number of magazines found in source   _____

    c. Percent of magazines found in source   _____

$$\frac{b \times 100}{a}$$

C. Audiovisual Materials

Source Title _____

    a. Number of AV items in sample   _____

    b. Number of AV items found in source   _____

    c. Percent of AV items found in source   _____

$$\frac{b \times 100}{a}$$

Figure 9. Comparison to Specialized Sources

Text or Index used _____

    a. Number of titles listed in text or index   _____

    b. Number of titles found in collection   _____

    c. Percent of titles found in collection   _____

$$\frac{b \times 100}{a}$$

Figure 10. Comparison to School Textbook/Periodicals Index

Teacher's name _____

Curricular area _____

Material needed _____

                    _____

                    _____

Reason unable to supply or slow to obtain material

_____

_____

_____

Will this unit of study be repeated, and the material needed again at a later date?

       _____ yes

       _____ probably

       _____ no

       _____ don't know

Figure 11. Unmet Teacher/Curricular Need

Special area of study _____

Total number of items included _____

Average age (see Figure 6) _____

Amount of use (see Figure 7) _____

Standard source used for comparison

_____

Number of items found _____

Percent of items found (see Figure 8) _____

Figure 12. Limited Areas for Evaluation

1. School name _____

2. Number of students in school _____

3. Annual media center budget _____
   Amount budgeted per pupil _____

4. Number of books in media center _____
   Number of books per pupil _____

5. Growth rate
   Number of titles added last year _____
   Number of titles lost/weeded last year _____
   Number of AV items added last year _____
   Number of AV items lost/weeded last year _____

6. Average collection age _____

7. Collection circulation figures
   Percent used this year _____
   Percent used last year, and not this year _____
   Percent used before last year and not since _____
   Percent not used _____

8. Comparison to standard sources
   Percent found in general source _____
   Percent found in magazine source _____
   Percent found in reference source _____
   Percent found in AV source _____
   Percent of textbook titles found _____

9. Limited area investigated
   Total number of items investigated _____
   Average age _____
   Amount of use _____
   Standard source used _____
   Percent found in standard source _____

10. Number of unmet teacher or curriculum requests ____
School Media Specialist _____

Figure 13. Summary Sheet—Collection Evaluation

	Number of Titles Dropped	Resulting Average Collection Age (From Fig. 6)	Estimated Replacement Cost (From Fig. 15)
First Calculation	None	_____	None
Second Calculation	_____	_____	_____
Third Calculation	_____	_____	_____
Fourth Calculation	_____	_____	_____
Fifth Calculation	_____	_____	_____

Figure 14. Cost to Lower Average Collection Age

	Second Calculation	Third Calculation	Fourth Calculation	Fifth Calculation
a. Number of Titles Dropped from Sample	_____	_____	_____	_____
b. Total Sample Size	_____	_____	_____	_____
c. Quotient $(a \div b)$	_____	_____	_____	_____
d. Total Collection Size	_____	_____	_____	_____
e. Number of Items to Be Replaced $(c \times d)$	_____	_____	_____	_____
f. Average Cost per Item	_____	_____	_____	_____
g. Estimated Replacement Cost $(e \times f)$	_____	_____	_____	_____

Figure 15. Estimated Replacement Cost

a. Amount of Money Available   _____

b. Average Cost per Item   _____

c. Number of Items to Be Purchased $(a \div b)$ _____

d. Total Collection Size   _____

e. Quotient $(c \div d)$ _____

f. Sample Size   _____

g. Number of Sample Titles to Be Replaced $(e \times f)$ _____

Figure 16. Estimate of Sample Items to Be Replaced

Amount of Money Available	Number of Sample Titles Dropped (From Figure 16)	Resulting Average Collection Age (From Figure 6)
_____	_____	_____

Figure 17. Effect of Money on Average Collection Age

| | Will it be needed again? | | | |
Material	Yes	Probably	No	Don't Know
Books	_____	_____	_____	_____
Audiovisual Items	_____	_____	_____	_____
Periodicals	_____	_____	_____	_____
Reference Materials	_____	_____	_____	_____

Figure 18. Number of Unmet Teacher/Curricular Needs

Item	Number of Items to Purchase	Average Cost Per Item*	Estimated Cost
_____	_____	_____	_____
_____	_____	_____	_____
_____	_____	_____	_____

*This information can be obtained from the *Library and Book Trade Almanac*, formerly the *Bowker Annual*.

Figure 19. Estimated Cost of Meeting Teacher Needs

a. Sample time   _____

b. Sample size   _____

c. Total collection size   _____

d. Quotient (line c ÷ line b)   _____

e. Product or estimated time

   (line d × line a)   _____

Figure 20. Estimating from Sample Times to Entire Collection

a. Number of sample titles to be weeded   _____

b. Sample size   _____

c. Total collection size   _____

d. Quotient (line a ÷ line b)   _____

e. Product or number of books to be weeded

   (line d × line c)   _____

Figure 21. Estimated Number of Titles or Volumes to Be Weeded

Selected
Bibliography

American Association of School Librarians and Association for Educational Communications and Technology. *Information Power: Guidelines for School Library Media Programs*. Chicago: American Library Association, 1988.

Chelton, Mary Kay. "Evaluation of Children's Materials." *Top of the News* (Winter 1987):463–84.

Gault, Robin. "Performance Measures for Evaluating Public Library Children's Services." *Public Libraries* (Winter 1984):134–37.

Hippenhammer, Craighton. "Managing Children's Library Collections through Objective Data." *Top of the News* (Spring 1986):309–13.

Library and Book Trade Annual (formerly the *Bowker Annual*). New York: Bowker.

Loertscher, David V., ed. *Measures of Excellence for School Library Media Centers*. Englewood, Colo.: Libraries Unlimited, 1988. Also in *Drexel Library Quarterly* (November 1986).

Miller, Marilyn L. and Marilyn L. Schontz. "Expenditures for Resources in School Library Media Centers, FY '88–'89." *School Library Journal* (June 1989):31–40.

Zweizig, Douglas L., Joan A. Braune, and Gloria Waity. *Output Measures for Children's Services in Wisconsin Public Libraries*. Madison, Wisc.: School of Library and Information Studies, 1989. (Available from Publications Office, UW-Madison SLIS, 600 North Park Street, Madison WI 53706 for $5.00.)

Carol A. Doll is an assistant professor at the Graduate School of Library and Information Science at the University of Washington. She is the author of *Evaluating Educational Software* (ALA, 1987) and *Using Informational Books in the Classroom* (Libraries Unlimited, 1990). An active member of the American Association of School Librarians, she has served as a member of the Secondary School Materials Selections Committee and Development of Critical Thinking Skills Committee. Doll received her doctorate from the University of Illinois.

Pamela Petrick Barron is an assistant professor in the College of Library and Information Science at the University of South Carolina. She was the content and research supervisor for "Jump over the Moon: Sharing Literature with Young Children," an award-winning, fifteen-part telecourse currently in use in the United States, Canada, and Europe. She is also the author, with Jennifer Burley, of *Jump over the Moon: Selected Professional Readings* (Holt, 1984), and co-author, with Patricia E. Seehan, of *Writers on Writing for Young Adults* (Omnigraphics, 1990). An active member of AASL and ALSC, she has served as a member of the AASL Critical Thinking Skills Committee and the ALSC 1990 Caldecott Committee. Barron received her doctorate from Florida State University.